ARRIVAL BEFORE DEPARTURE:

A practical guide for building wealth and securing a comfortable future.

Matthew L. Copeland.

Dedication:

I dedicate this book to God for His matchless and enabling grace. Dedicated to my family, whose love and constant support made this book possible. Dedicated to all those aspiring to build wealth and secure a comfortable future. Your resilience and commitment inspire this book. May this guide be a beacon on your path to financial success.

- Laying the groundwork for the life-changing adventure.
- Seed of Departure.
- Adventure across Areas.
- Investigating personal development and self-discovery.
- Chronicles of Anticipation: Stories of those who arrived before departing.
- Methods of self-discovering before embarking on journeys beyond oneself.

- Intersecting Paths.
- Moment of Intersection.
- Family and Relationship Intersection.
- Educational Expenses, Student loans and the long-term impact on wealth accumulation.

- Crafting Your time for early success.
- Reaching your destination ahead of schedule.
- Methods for efficiently managing your time.

- The Challenge of balancing immediate need with long term Objectives.
- The need for financial preparedness during Job changes or Advancement.
- Strategies for managing short-term financial demand without compromising the achievement of long-term goals.

In a world defined by constant change and uncertainty, the pursuit of financial stability and prosperity stands as a paramount endeavor. "Arrival before Departure" is a comprehensive exploration of the strategies, principles, and insights essential to navigating the complex landscape of personal finance. As we embark on this journey together, the book serves as a roadmap, offering practical advice and timeless wisdom to empower you in achieving lasting financial success. It's not just about reaching your destination; it's about arriving well-prepared before the journey's end.

Chapter 1.

Loosening up the Beginning stages.

Laying the groundwork for the life-changing adventure.

In the journey of life, the concept of "Arrival before Departure" serves as a guiding principle for those seeking financial stability and a comfortable future. This life-changing adventure involves strategic planning, disciplined actions, and a commitment to long-term goals. In this practical guide, we will explore the essential steps to lay the groundwork for building wealth and ensuring a secure future.

1. Define Your Financial Destination:

Before embarking on any journey, it's crucial to define your destination. Similarly, in the pursuit of wealth, setting clear financial goals is the first step. Whether it's buying a home, funding education, or retiring comfortably, outlining your objectives provides a roadmap for your financial journey.

2. Budgeting:

Budgeting is the compass that keeps you on the right path. Track your income, expenses, and savings diligently. Creating a realistic budget ensures that you allocate funds wisely, allowing you to save and invest for the future while meeting your current needs.

3. Emergency Fund:

Life is unpredictable, and unexpected expenses can derail your financial plans. Building an emergency fund is like having a safety net. Aim for three to six months' worth of living expenses in a liquid, easily accessible account to cushion any financial shocks.

4. Debt Management:
High-interest debts can hinder your progress. Develop a plan to pay off outstanding debts systematically, starting with those carrying the highest interest rates. Being debt-free opens up avenues for wealth accumulation.

5. Invest Wisely:
Investing is a powerful tool for wealth creation. Diversify your investments across different asset classes such as stocks, bonds, and real estate. Consider consulting with a financial advisor to tailor an investment strategy that aligns with your goals, risk tolerance, and timeline.

6. Retirement Planning:
Arriving before departure also means preparing for the later stages of life. Contribute regularly to retirement accounts like 401(k)s or IRAs. Take advantage of employer-

sponsored plans and ensure that you are on track to maintain a comfortable lifestyle during retirement.

7. Continuous Learning:

Financial literacy is the cornerstone of building wealth. Stay informed about personal finance, investment strategies, and economic trends. Attend workshops, read books, and leverage online resources to enhance your financial knowledge.

8. Real Estate:

Owning property can be a significant asset. Consider real estate as part of your wealth-building strategy. Whether it's a primary residence or investment property, real estate has the potential for long-term appreciation.

9. Insurance Coverage:

Protecting your assets is as crucial as accumulating them. Obtain appropriate insurance coverage for health, life, property, and income protection. Insurance provides a safety net, ensuring that unforeseen events do not jeopardize your financial stability.

10. Estate Planning:
Secure your legacy by engaging in estate planning. Draft a will, designate beneficiaries, and consider trusts to ensure a smooth transition of assets to your heirs. Estate planning is a vital component of the arrival-before-departure philosophy.

In conclusion, the journey to financial prosperity is a well-planned adventure. "Arrival before Departure" is not merely about accumulating wealth; it's about making strategic choices today to secure a comfortable future. By defining your financial goals, managing debt, investing wisely, and staying informed, you lay the groundwork for a life-changing journey toward financial success. Embrace this practical guide, and you'll find yourself arriving at a future destination filled with financial security and peace of mind.

Seeds of Departure.

In the intricate tapestry of life, the concept of departure often carries a weighty significance. It signifies the beginning of a new journey, the start of something different. This profound notion is intricately woven into the fabric of the book, "Arrival before Departure", In this book, we delve into the seeds of departure sown within the pages of this enlightening guide, exploring the wealth-building principles that empower readers to shape their destinies.

Understanding the Seeds

The metaphorical seeds of departure represent the foundational principles that propel individuals towards financial prosperity and a secure future. The book advocates for proactive decision-making, urging readers to plant these seeds in the fertile soil of their lives to cultivate a bountiful harvest in the years to come.

Financial Literacy:

Central to the book's philosophy is the seed of financial literacy. Just as a seed needs nourishment to sprout, individuals require knowledge about managing finances to lay the groundwork for prosperity. "Arrival before Departure" serves as a guide, offering insights into budgeting, investing, and understanding the nuances of financial markets.

Investment Strategies:
The seeds of departure take root in the realm of investment strategies. The book advocates for a diversified and thoughtful approach to investments. By sowing the seeds of informed decision-making in various investment avenues, readers can weather financial storms and reap the benefits of a well-cultivated portfolio.

Entrepreneurial Mindset:
Departure often involves stepping into the unknown, and the book encourages readers to embrace an entrepreneurial mindset. Sowing seeds of innovation and risk-taking can lead to the growth of personal ventures, potentially creating new avenues for wealth generation.

Cultivating the Seeds

The book not only introduces these seeds of departure but also provides actionable steps to cultivate them effectively.

Goal Setting:
Just as a gardener envisions a vibrant garden before planting seeds, the book guides readers in setting clear financial goals.

Whether it's homeownership, retirement, or educational endeavors, defining objectives becomes the compass that directs the cultivation of these seeds.

Discipline and Patience:

Cultivating seeds requires discipline and patience. "Arrival before Departure" emphasizes the importance of sticking to a financial plan and patiently nurturing investments over time. This disciplined approach ensures a steady growth trajectory and guards against impulsive decisions that could hinder financial prosperity.

Adaptability:

Just as a well-tended garden adapts to changing seasons, financial strategies need to be adaptable. The book encourages readers to embrace change, learn from experiences, and adjust their financial plans accordingly. This adaptability is key to navigating the dynamic landscape of personal finance.

Harvesting the Fruits:

The ultimate aim of sowing the seeds of departure is to harvest the fruits of financial success and a comfortable future. The book provides readers with a roadmap to reap these rewards through practical tips and real-life examples.

Wealth Accumulation:

By diligently following the principles outlined in the book, readers can accumulate wealth over time. Whether through smart investments, entrepreneurial pursuits, or strategic savings, the seeds planted earlier blossom into a financial harvest that provides security and peace of mind.

Legacy Building:

Departure also signifies leaving a legacy. The book prompts readers to think beyond their immediate financial goals and consider how their wealth can positively impact future generations. By sowing seeds of departure with a generational perspective, individuals can leave a lasting legacy for their families.

Conclusion:

In the journey of life, departure is inevitable, but with strategic planning and the cultivation of the seeds of departure outlined in "Arrival before Departure," individuals can shape their financial destinies. The book serves as a compass, guiding readers through the intricacies of wealth-building, ensuring that their departure is not a leap into uncertainty but a well-prepared step towards a comfortable and prosperous future.

Adventure Across Areas

In the captivating realm of financial literacy and future security, this book, "Arrival before Departure" serves as a compass for those seeking to embark on a transformative adventure across various areas of life. This adventure is not just about accumulating wealth; it's a comprehensive journey that encompasses financial, personal, and professional aspects, creating a harmonious tapestry for a secure and fulfilling future.
Diversification as the Gateway to Financial Adventure:
One of the key areas explored in this book is the concept of diversification. Just as a seasoned

adventurer explores different terrains to enhance their skills, diversifying one's financial portfolio involves spreading investments across various asset classes. This strategy not only mitigates risk but also opens up avenues for growth in different market conditions. Your guide encourages readers to navigate the financial landscape with agility, balancing risk and reward as they traverse the diverse terrains of stocks, bonds, real estate, and other investment vehicles.

Navigating the Terrain of Income Streams:

The adventure across areas is not solely restricted to financial investments. This book wisely delves into the significance of multiple income streams as a means of fortifying one's financial fortress. By encouraging readers to explore various sources of income – be it through entrepreneurship, investments, or side hustles – you guide them in creating a resilient financial ecosystem. This not only safeguards against unexpected challenges but also enhances the potential for wealth accumulation.

Cultivating the Garden of Personal Growth:

Beyond the financial domain, this book advocates for personal development as an integral part of the adventure. Much like an explorer honing survival skills, individuals are urged to invest in their education, skills, and well-being. The narrative intertwines the financial journey with personal growth, emphasizing that the synergy between the two is crucial for a holistic approach to securing a comfortable future.

Professional Expedition: Career Development and Entrepreneurship:

The expedition across areas extends to the professional realm. This book encourages readers to view their careers as a dynamic landscape, ripe for exploration and growth. Whether through climbing the corporate ladder or venturing into entrepreneurship, individuals are inspired to navigate their professional terrain strategically. By providing practical insights and actionable advice, you empower readers to make informed decisions that align with their long-term goals.

Navigating the Terrain of Risk Management:

Every adventurer encounters obstacles, and the financial journey is no exception. This book serves as a guide through the treacherous terrain of risk management. By fostering an understanding of risks and teaching effective risk mitigation strategies, readers are equipped to navigate uncertainties with resilience and confidence. This comprehensive approach ensures that the adventure remains on course, regardless of the challenges encountered along the way.

Building a Legacy Across Generations:

The adventure across areas is not solely for personal gain but extends to building a lasting legacy. This book advocates for generational wealth as the pinnacle of the journey, emphasizing the importance of passing down financial wisdom and resources to future generations. By instilling a mindset of stewardship, you inspire readers to view wealth as a tool for positive impact, creating a legacy that transcends individual accomplishments.

Conclusion:

In "Arrival before Departure" you've crafted a roadmap for an all-encompassing adventure that goes beyond mere financial success. It's a journey that requires courage, strategic planning, and a commitment to continuous growth. By navigating the diverse areas of finance, personal development, and professional exploration, readers are not just accumulating wealth – they are crafting a future that is secure, fulfilling, and rich with possibilities. As they embark on this transformative adventure, this book serves as a trusted guide, illuminating the path to a life of prosperity and contentment.

Investigating personal development and self-discovery.

In the pursuit of wealth and a secure future, it's easy to get caught up in the external factors of financial planning and investment strategies. However, the foundation for a prosperous life extends beyond monetary considerations. "Arrival before Departure," your practical guide to building wealth, recognizes the importance of personal development and self-discovery as integral elements in the journey towards a comfortable future.

Understanding the Connection: Personal Development and Wealth Building

The link between personal development and building wealth is often underestimated. In this book, you delve into the concept that true wealth is not only about financial prosperity but also encompasses a holistic approach to self-improvement. Personal development acts as the catalyst for achieving financial goals, creating a synergy that propels individuals towards success.

The Power of Self-Reflection in Achieving Financial Goals

"Arrival before Departure" encourages readers to embark on a journey of self-discovery, emphasizing the role of self-reflection in shaping one's financial destiny. By understanding personal strengths, weaknesses, and values, individuals can align their financial pursuits with their authentic selves. This alignment not only leads to more meaningful financial decisions but also contributes to a sense of fulfillment and purpose.

Setting Meaningful Goals: Aligning Personal and Financial Objectives

This book highlights the significance of setting goals that go beyond mere monetary achievements. It emphasizes the need to align financial objectives with personal aspirations, fostering a harmonious connection between the pursuit of wealth and one's deeper sense of purpose. By incorporating personal development into the goal-setting process, individuals can create a roadmap that not only secures financial stability but also enhances overall life satisfaction.

Overcoming Limiting Beliefs: A Crucial Step in Personal Development

In the journey towards wealth creation, addressing limiting

beliefs is paramount. "Arrival before Departure" guides readers to identify and overcome self-imposed barriers that may hinder financial success. By fostering a mindset of abundance and cultivating a positive self-image, individuals can unlock their full potential, paving the way for greater achievements in both personal and financial realms.

Cultivating Financial Intelligence through Self-Education.

While financial literacy is a cornerstone of wealth building, this book acknowledges that personal development extends to continuous self-education. Encouraging readers to stay informed about economic trends, investment opportunities, and financial strategies, "Arrival before Departure" promotes a proactive approach to learning. This commitment to ongoing education empowers individuals to make informed decisions, adapt to changing circumstances, and optimize their financial growth.

Building Resilience in the Face of Challenges

The path to financial success is rarely without challenges. This book recognizes the importance of resilience in overcoming setbacks and adapting to unforeseen circumstances. Personal development plays a pivotal role in building resilience, equipping individuals with the mental and emotional strength needed to navigate financial uncertainties. By embracing challenges as opportunities for growth, readers of "Arrival before Departure" can fortify their journey towards wealth and security.

Balancing Ambition and Well-Being: The Holistic Approach to Success

"Arrival before Departure" advocates for a balanced approach to success that considers not only financial achievements but also well-being. Acknowledging the interconnectedness of physical, mental, and financial health, the book encourages readers to cultivate a holistic lifestyle. Balancing ambition with self-care fosters sustained success, ensuring that individuals not only arrive at their financial destinations but also enjoy the journey along the way.

Conclusion: Integrating Personal Development into the Wealth-Building Journey

In conclusion, this book "Arrival before Departure" presents a compelling argument for the integration of personal development and self-discovery into the pursuit of wealth. By recognizing the interconnected nature of personal and financial well-being, readers are guided towards a more fulfilling and prosperous life. As individuals embark on the journey outlined in your practical guide, they not only secure a comfortable future but also uncover the profound richness that comes from aligning their financial pursuits with their authentic selves.

Chronicles of Anticipation: Stories of Those Who Arrived Before Departing.

In the vast landscape of personal development and financial literature, a unique and intriguing concept has emerged — "Arrival before departure." This idea is not just a catchy phrase; it's a philosophy that resonates with those who seek to build wealth and secure a comfortable future. As we delve into the Chronicles of Anticipation, we will explore the stories of individuals who have embodied this philosophy and achieved success by arriving at their goals before departing from the norm.

Part 1: The Essence of Arrival Before Departure

To understand the concept fully, we must first grasp its essence. "Arrival before departure" is not about rushing through life but rather about anticipation and strategic planning. It's a mindset that encourages individuals to envision their desired destination and work tirelessly towards reaching it before conventional timelines. In the realm of financial success, this means building wealth and securing a comfortable future sooner rather than later.

Part 2: The Trailblazers

The Chronicles of Anticipation are filled with stories of trailblazers who defied societal norms and achieved remarkable success. Take the story of

Richard Anderson, a visionary entrepreneur who, in his early 30s, built a multimillion-dollar tech company. By diligently investing, saving, and making strategic career moves, Anderson arrived at financial independence long before his peers. His story serves as an inspiration for those who choose to embark on their journey toward wealth early in life.

Part 3: The Power of Delayed Gratification

At the heart of "Arrival before departure" lies the power of delayed gratification. Many individuals featured in the Chronicles share a common thread — the ability to resist immediate pleasures for long-term gains. Sarah Mitchell, a finance professional, exemplifies this principle. Instead of succumbing to the allure of instant gratification, Mitchell chose to save and invest consistently throughout her career. As a result, she now enjoys financial security and the freedom to pursue her passions.

Part 4: Strategic Investments and Planning.

Building wealth requires more than just hard work; it demands strategic investments and meticulous planning. The Chronicles highlight stories of individuals who mastered the art of financial planning. Jason Turner, a real estate investor, strategically acquired properties during market downturns, capitalizing on opportunities that others overlooked. Turner's story underscores the importance of strategic foresight in the journey toward financial success.

Part 5: Overcoming Challenges and Adversities

The path to arrival before departure is not without challenges. The Chronicles share stories of resilience and determination, showcasing individuals who overcame setbacks to achieve their financial goals. Maria Rodriguez, a single mother, faced numerous challenges but remained steadfast in her commitment to building a secure future for her family. Through hard work and perseverance, Rodriguez not only secured her family's comfort but also became an advocate for financial literacy in her community.

Part 6: Lessons for the Next Generation

As we explore the Chronicles of Anticipation, it becomes clear that the stories within are not just for the present but also for the future. The lessons learned from these individuals serve as a guide for the next generation of aspiring wealth builders. Encouraging young minds to embrace the philosophy of arrival before departure sets the stage for a society that prioritizes financial literacy, planning, and responsible decision-making.

Conclusion:

The Chronicles of Anticipation paint a vivid picture of individuals who dared to dream, plan strategically, and achieve financial success ahead of their time. The concept of arrival before departure is not a sprint but a marathon, requiring dedication, discipline, and a forward-thinking mindset. As we reflect on these stories, it becomes evident that the journey toward building wealth and securing a comfortable future is not confined to a specific age or stage in life. It is a journey that anyone can embark upon with the right mindset, perseverance, and a commitment to arriving at their destination before departing from their financial aspirations.

Methods for self-discovery before embarking on Journeys beyond oneself:

In the pursuit of building wealth and securing a comfortable future, it is essential to embark on a journey of self-discovery. The concept of self-discovery goes beyond the conventional understanding of personal growth; it is the compass that guides us through the intricate paths of life, helping us make informed decisions that align with our true selves. This book explores various methods for self-discovery before venturing into the realm of financial success, as discussed in the book "Arrival before Departure: Practical guide for building wealth and securing a comfortable future."

Reflection and Introspection:

Before setting out on any journey, it is crucial to reflect on one's values, passions, and long-term goals. Take the time to introspect and understand what truly matters to you. Consider the values that will guide your financial decisions and shape your path to wealth. This method involves journaling, meditation, or simply spending quiet moments contemplating your aspirations.

Financial Personality Assessment:

Understanding your financial personality is a key aspect of self-discovery in the context of wealth building. The book advocates for tools and assessments that help individuals identify their attitudes towards money, risk tolerance, and spending habits. By gaining insights into your financial personality, you can tailor your wealth-building strategies to align with your strengths and mitigate potential challenges.

Goal Setting and Vision Boarding:

Set clear, realistic financial goals that align with your aspirations. Create a vision board that visually represents your desired future, including financial milestones, lifestyle choices, and personal achievements. This method not only helps in clarifying your objectives but also serves as a constant reminder of the destination you are working towards.

Skills and Talents Inventory: Identifying and leveraging your skills and talents is fundamental to self-discovery. The book suggests conducting a comprehensive inventory of your abilities, both professional and personal. By recognizing your strengths, you can identify opportunities for personal and financial growth. This process can also uncover potential income streams that align with your passions and skills.

Risk and Resilience Assessment: Financial success often involves navigating uncertainties and taking calculated risks. Assessing your risk tolerance and developing resilience strategies is crucial before venturing into wealth-building endeavors. The book encourages readers to evaluate their comfort levels with financial risks and devise coping mechanisms to bounce back from setbacks.

Networking and Mentorship:

Engaging with a diverse network of individuals and seeking mentorship is a powerful method for self-discovery. The book emphasizes the importance of surrounding oneself with like-minded individuals who share similar financial goals. Mentorship provides valuable insights, guidance, and a support system that can accelerate your journey towards building wealth.

Embracing Continuous Learning:

Self-discovery is an ongoing process, and the pursuit of knowledge is a vital component. The book encourages readers to invest in their education, stay informed about financial trends, and continuously acquire new skills. This commitment to learning not only enhances your capabilities but also keeps you adaptable in an ever-evolving economic landscape.

Conclusion:

Embarking on journeys beyond oneself, particularly in the realm of financial success, requires a solid foundation of self-discovery. The methods discussed in "Arrival before Departure: Practical guide for building wealth and securing a comfortable future" provide a roadmap for individuals to understand themselves better, align their financial endeavors with their true selves, and navigate the path to a prosperous and fulfilling future. As you venture into the world of wealth-building, remember that true success begins with self-discovery.

In the journey of life, the concepts of arrival and departure take center stage. These notions, often associated with travel, also play a crucial role in the realm of personal finance and wealth-building. In the context of the book "Arrival before Departure" the theme of convergence emerges as a powerful and transformative concept. This book explores the significance of convergence, examining how the intersection of arrival and departure can pave the way for financial success and a secure future.

Understanding Arrival and Departure.

Arrival signifies the attainment of goals, milestones, and financial prosperity. It is the destination we aim for, representing the culmination of hard work, strategic planning, and perseverance. Departure, on the other hand, embodies the beginning of a new journey or phase. It involves leaving behind the familiar, embracing change, and adapting to new circumstances. Together, arrival and departure form the dynamic cycle of personal and financial growth.

Convergence: The Interplay of Goals and Strategies

Convergence occurs when the objectives outlined in "Arrival before Departure" align seamlessly with the strategies employed to achieve them. It is the strategic coming together of financial goals and the actions taken to realize them. Convergence involves a harmonious blend of long-term planning, disciplined execution, and adaptability to changing circumstances. One key aspect of convergence is the synchronization of short-term and long-term goals. The book emphasizes the importance of setting achievable milestones on the path to long-term financial success. These smaller goals serve as checkpoints, allowing individuals to celebrate achievements, reassess strategies, and make necessary adjustments.

Investment Strategies and Convergence

The convergence of arrival and departure is particularly evident in the realm of investments. Smart investment decisions, as advocated in the book, contribute significantly to the convergence of financial goals. Diversification, risk management, and a focus on long-term growth are integral components of an effective investment strategy.

The book encourages readers to view investments not merely as financial tools but as vehicles driving them towards their desired destination. By aligning investments with personal financial goals, individuals can experience the convergence of their wealth-building efforts and the realization of their aspirations.

Adaptability and Resilience

Convergence also involves adaptability and resilience in the face of challenges. The journey towards financial success is rarely a straight path; it often involves detours, unexpected setbacks, and economic fluctuations. The book underscores the importance of embracing change, learning from failures, and adjusting strategies to stay on course.

Arrival before departure is not just about accumulating wealth; it's about securing a comfortable future. Convergence, in this context, means being adaptable to the evolving landscape of personal finance and making informed decisions that align with long-term objectives.

The Role of Financial Education

A crucial aspect of achieving convergence is fostering financial literacy. The book emphasizes the significance of understanding fundamental financial principles, empowering readers to make informed decisions. Financial education serves as a compass, guiding individuals through the convergence of arrival and departure by providing them with the knowledge and tools needed to navigate the complexities of wealth-building.

Planning for Departure: Legacy and Impact

While arrival is associated with personal success, departure introduces the concept of legacy and impact. The book encourages readers to consider the broader implications of their financial decisions on future generations. Convergence, in this context, involves aligning personal financial goals with the desire to leave a positive legacy and make a meaningful impact on the lives of others.

Conclusion

In the realm of personal finance, convergence is the bridge that connects arrival and departure. It is the strategic alignment of financial goals with the actions taken to achieve them. "Arrival before Departure" serves as a roadmap, guiding readers towards the convergence of their aspirations and the practical steps required to attain them. By embracing the principles outlined in the book, individuals can navigate the journey of wealth-building with purpose, resilience, and a clear vision of their desired destination.

Intersecting Paths

In the journey of life, our paths often intersect with various opportunities and challenges. Much like the themes explored in the book "Arrival before Departure" the concept of intersecting paths plays a pivotal role in shaping our financial destinies. This book delves into the intricate web of choices, decisions, and unforeseen circumstances that intertwine as individuals navigate their quest for financial success.

Section 1: Navigating Financial Crossroads:

Life is a series of crossroads where financial decisions can significantly impact our future. The book "Arrival before Departure" serves as a compass, guiding readers through the complexities of these intersections. Whether it's choosing a career path, making investment decisions, or planning for retirement, the book provides practical insights on how to navigate these crucial moments and make informed choices.

Section 2: Building Wealth through Convergence

Wealth-building is often a result of strategic convergence – the alignment of various elements in our financial journey. "Arrival before Departure" explores the idea that true wealth is not merely monetary but encompasses a holistic approach that integrates financial stability, personal fulfillment, and meaningful relationships. This section examines how these intersecting paths can lead to a more fulfilling and prosperous life.

Section 3: Seizing Opportunities at the Crossroads

Opportunities are fleeting, and recognizing them at the crossroads of life is a skill honed by the wise. The book emphasizes the importance of being prepared to seize these opportunities when they present themselves. Whether it's a career move, an investment prospect, or a chance to cultivate new skills, the intersecting paths in one's journey can lead to transformative opportunities for wealth creation.

Section 4: Mitigating Risks through Intersectional Planning

Just as opportunities arise, challenges and risks are inevitable. "Arrival before Departure" advocates for proactive planning to mitigate risks effectively. This section explores how intersectional planning – considering the convergence of various financial elements – can safeguard one's wealth and provide a secure foundation for the future.

Section 5: The Journey of Self-Discovery

Intersecting paths aren't solely about financial decisions; they also encompass self-discovery.

The book encourages readers to reflect on their values, passions, and long-term goals. By understanding oneself better, individuals can align their financial paths with their personal aspirations, leading to a more purposeful and gratifying journey.

Conclusion:

"Arrival before Departure" invites readers to view their financial journey as a series of intersecting paths. Through insightful guidance and practical strategies, the book empowers individuals to navigate these intersections with confidence and purpose. As we traverse the crossroads of life, the wisdom imparted in the book becomes a beacon, illuminating the way to a future of financial prosperity and personal fulfillment.

Moments of Intersection

Moment of Intersection in the context of financial decisions refers to critical points in time where various factors converge, leading to significant implications for one's financial strategy. These moments often mark a juncture where key elements intersect, requiring careful consideration and informed decision-making. Exploring this concept involves understanding the interplay of various factors that influence financial choices.

One pivotal moment of intersection occurs when balancing short-term gains against long-term goals. Individuals often face the dilemma of immediate financial gratification versus the discipline of saving for future needs. This intersection prompts a reflection on priorities, risk tolerance, and the trade-offs between instant rewards and sustained financial well-being.

Investment decisions also encounter moments of intersection, especially when assessing market trends, economic conditions, and personal financial objectives. Investors must navigate the convergence of factors such as market volatility, interest rates, and global events to make informed choices. Recognizing these moments of intersection allows for strategic adjustments to investment portfolios, aligning them with evolving market dynamics.

Similarly, life events like marriage, parenthood, or career changes introduce moments of intersection in financial planning. These transitions require a reassessment of financial goals, budgeting strategies, and risk management. The intersection of personal milestones with financial decisions necessitates a dynamic approach to adapt to changing circumstances.

The intersection of technology and finance is another critical juncture in the contemporary landscape. The rise of digital currencies, fintech innovations, and online financial platforms introduces new possibilities and risks. Individuals must navigate this intersection by staying informed about technological advancements, understanding the implications for traditional financial systems, and making decisions that align with their financial objectives.

Economic downturns or recessions represent profound moments of intersection that impact financial decisions on a macroeconomic scale. During these periods, individuals must navigate challenges such as job insecurity, market downturns, and changing interest rates. Successful financial navigation at these intersections involves prudent planning, diversification, and adaptability to economic shifts.

The intersection of personal values and financial decisions is a crucial aspect often overlooked. Aligning financial choices with one's values involves considering ethical investments, sustainable practices, and socially responsible financial decisions. This intersection reflects a growing awareness of the broader impact of financial choices on both individual well-being and the greater community.

In conclusion, moments of intersection in financial decisions encapsulate critical junctures where various factors converge, demanding thoughtful analysis and strategic decision-making. These intersections encompass a broad spectrum, from personal milestones to economic shifts and technological advancements. Navigating these moments requires a dynamic and informed approach that considers the interplay of short-term gains, long-term goals, market dynamics, personal values, and the ever-changing financial landscape. By recognizing and effectively addressing these moments of intersection, individuals can make sound financial decisions that align with their objectives and withstand the complexities of an ever-evolving financial world.

How pivotal life moments intersect with financial choices:

Life is an intricate tapestry woven with pivotal moments that shape our journey. From the joyous occasions to the challenging crossroads, each experience influences the decisions we make, particularly in the realm of finances. In this exploration, we delve into the interconnected web of pivotal life moments and the financial choices that often accompany them.

Educational Milestones:

The pursuit of education is a monumental journey marked by key milestones. Whether it's choosing a college, pursuing advanced degrees, or entering the workforce, these moments significantly impact financial trajectories. The decision to invest in education often involves navigating student loans, scholarships, and long-term financial planning. Balancing the pursuit of knowledge with fiscal responsibility becomes a critical aspect of these crossroads.

Career Transitions:

Changing careers or embracing new professional opportunities represents another juncture where life and finances intersect. From job relocations to entrepreneurship ventures, individuals face decisions that carry financial implications. The need for strategic financial planning becomes evident as one navigates salary negotiations, investment in skills development, and the potential risks associated with career transitions.

Marriage and Family Planning:

The decision to embark on a journey of partnership and family introduces a new layer of financial considerations. From planning weddings to securing a home and preparing for the financial responsibilities of parenthood, individuals must navigate the delicate balance between personal aspirations and shared financial goals. Open communication and joint financial planning play a pivotal role in this intersection of life and finance.

Health Challenges:

Facing health challenges is an inevitable part of life's journey. Whether it's unexpected medical expenses, long-term care planning, or insurance considerations, health-related pivotal moments demand careful financial navigation. Establishing emergency funds, evaluating insurance coverage, and making informed healthcare decisions become integral components of managing the financial fallout from health crises.

Retirement Planning:

As individuals approach the later stages of their careers, the prospect of retirement becomes a central focus. Deciding when to retire, assessing pension options, and planning for post-retirement lifestyles require meticulous financial planning. The intersection of life's accumulated experiences and financial foresight becomes evident as individuals seek to maintain a comfortable and secure retirement.

Conclusion:

In the intricate dance of life, pivotal moments and financial choices are inextricably linked. The decisions made at each crossroad reverberate through one's financial landscape, shaping the future and influencing subsequent life milestones. By recognizing the intersection of these aspects, individuals can embark on a journey of holistic financial well-being, navigating the twists and turns with resilience and foresight.

Family and Relationship Intersection:

In the intricate web of our lives, the intersection of family dynamics and financial decisions often presents challenges and opportunities that shape our well-being. The delicate balance between individual aspirations and familial responsibilities becomes particularly pronounced when navigating the complex landscape of monetary choices. This book explores the multifaceted nature of family and relationship intersections in the context of financial decision-making.

Shared Financial Goals:

One of the crucial aspects of family finance is establishing shared financial goals. Whether planning for major life events, such as buying a home or funding a child's education, aligning goals within a family unit fosters a sense of unity and purpose. Clear communication and compromise are key elements in ensuring that individual aspirations harmonize with collective financial objectives.

Budgeting and Financial Planning:

Creating a comprehensive budget is fundamental to sound financial management within a family. It involves open discussions about income, expenses, and savings. Establishing a budget not only helps in managing day-to-day finances but also allows for setting aside funds for future endeavors. Collaborative financial planning strengthens the familial bond and promotes a sense of security.

Financial Transparency:

Transparency in financial matters is an essential component of a healthy relationship. Openly discussing income, debt, and spending habits builds trust and minimizes the potential for financial conflicts. Establishing a culture of transparency within a family sets the stage for informed decision-making and reinforces a shared commitment to financial well-being.

Roles and Responsibilities:

Defining roles and responsibilities in financial matters is crucial for avoiding misunderstandings and reducing stress. Whether it's managing bills, investments, or savings, a clear delineation of responsibilities ensures that each family member contributes to the overall financial health. This division of labor also promotes accountability and cooperation.

Navigating Financial Challenges: Life is unpredictable, and financial challenges are inevitable. Whether facing unexpected medical expenses, job loss, or other setbacks, the ability of a family to weather these storms is often a testament to their resilience. Open communication, adaptability, and a shared commitment to finding solutions are crucial during such trying times.

Educating the Next Generation: Instilling financial literacy in the younger generation is an investment in the family's future. Teaching children about budgeting, saving, and responsible spending empowers them to make informed financial decisions as they grow older. Family discussions about money can contribute to a positive financial mindset that extends through generations.

Balancing Autonomy and Interdependence: While shared financial goals are important, it's equally crucial to balance individual autonomy within a family. Allowing each member a degree of financial independence fosters a sense of empowerment and self-responsibility. Striking the right balance between autonomy and interdependence contributes to a harmonious financial ecosystem.

Couples and Money:

In romantic relationships, the intersection of love and money can be particularly intricate. Addressing financial differences early on, establishing shared financial goals, and maintaining open communication are essential for a healthy financial partnership. Negotiating financial decisions within a couple requires a blend of compromise, understanding, and shared values.

Conclusion:

In the tapestry of family life, financial decisions weave a narrative of shared dreams, challenges, and triumphs. Navigating the intersection of family dynamics and financial choices requires a commitment to open communication, shared goals, and mutual support. By embracing financial transparency, planning for the future, and fostering a culture of resilience, families can strengthen their bonds and build a foundation for lasting financial well-being.

Educational expenses, student loans, and the long-term impact on wealth accumulation.

Education is often considered a gateway to success, but the rising costs of higher education bring with them a significant financial burden. Planning for educational expenses, understanding student loans, and anticipating their long-term impact on wealth accumulation have become crucial aspects of financial management for students and their families.

The Rising Cost of Education

Over the past few decades, the cost of education has skyrocketed, outpacing inflation and wage growth. Tuition fees, accommodation, textbooks, and other miscellaneous expenses can accumulate quickly, putting a strain on both students and their families. Aspiring students are faced with the challenge of not only securing a spot in their desired institutions but also finding ways to fund their education without compromising their financial future.

Strategic Planning for Educational Expenses

To mitigate the financial strain of educational expenses, strategic planning is essential. This includes researching available scholarships, grants, and financial aid options. Additionally, setting up a dedicated savings fund well in advance can provide a financial cushion. Parents and students alike should explore cost-effective education alternatives, such as community colleges or vocational training programs, to balance academic aspirations with financial realities.

Navigating the World of Student Loans

For many students, taking out loans is an inevitable part of funding their education. Understanding the types of student loans available, interest rates, and repayment terms is crucial. Federal student loans often offer more favorable terms compared to private loans, including income-driven repayment plans and loan forgiveness options. Careful consideration of loan terms and their implications is vital to avoid falling into a cycle of debt that could hinder long-term financial goals.

Long-Term Impact on Wealth Accumulation.

Student loans can have a lasting impact on an individual's ability to accumulate wealth. High monthly loan payments can strain post-graduation budgets, limiting the capacity to save and invest. This can delay major life milestones such as homeownership and starting a family. The burden of student debt may also affect career choices, pushing individuals toward higher-paying but less personally fulfilling jobs to meet financial obligations.

Strategies for Managing Student Loan Debt

Successfully managing student loan debt requires a proactive approach. Creating a realistic budget that prioritizes debt repayment, exploring loan forgiveness programs, and considering refinancing options are all strategies that can alleviate the long-term financial impact. It's essential to stay informed about changes in legislation that may affect student loans and take advantage of any opportunities for relief.

Balancing Education and Wealth Goals

Balancing the pursuit of education with long-term wealth goals is a delicate act. While education is an investment in oneself, it is crucial to approach it with a clear understanding of the financial implications. Making informed decisions about educational expenses, utilizing financial aid wisely, and managing student loans responsibly contribute to a healthier financial future.

The Role of Financial Literacy

One of the key elements in navigating the complex landscape of educational expenses and student loans is financial literacy. Schools, colleges, and universities should prioritize incorporating financial education into their curriculum to empower students with the knowledge needed to make informed decisions. Additionally, individuals can seek guidance from financial advisors to ensure their strategies align with their broader financial goals.

Conclusion

Planning for educational expenses, understanding student loans, and mitigating their long-term impact on wealth accumulation require a combination of foresight, strategic decision-making, and financial literacy. By taking a proactive approach, individuals can pursue their educational aspirations while minimizing the financial burden that often comes with it. Ultimately, the intersection of education and financial well-being is a critical aspect of building a secure and prosperous future.

In the pursuit of financial success and a comfortable future, effective time management and clear objectives play crucial roles. The concept of "Arrival Before Departure" encapsulates the idea of planning and executing tasks efficiently to achieve financial goals. This book explores the importance of managing one's time and setting objectives in the context of building wealth and securing a comfortable future.

The Significance of Time Management:

Time is a finite resource, and how we utilize it can significantly impact our financial journey. Efficient time management allows individuals to maximize productivity, focus on key priorities, and allocate resources wisely. In the quest for financial success, every minute counts. By prioritizing tasks, setting realistic deadlines, and avoiding procrastination, one can create a structured approach to wealth building.

Setting Clear Objectives:

Clear objectives act as a roadmap towards financial success. Without a destination in mind, it's challenging to stay on course. Define short-term and long-term financial goals, whether it's saving for a home, investing in education, or building a retirement fund. Objectives provide a sense of direction, helping individuals make informed decisions and avoid distractions that may hinder wealth accumulation.

Creating a Time-Objectives Framework:

To effectively manage time and objectives, it's crucial to establish a personalized framework. Begin by identifying your priorities and breaking down larger financial goals into manageable tasks. Use tools such as calendars, planners, or digital apps to schedule activities, deadlines, and milestones. This framework acts as a visual guide, aiding in the organization and execution of tasks necessary for wealth building.

Prioritizing High-Impact Activities:

Not all tasks contribute equally to financial success. Identify high-impact activities that directly align with your objectives. Focus on activities that generate income, enhance skills, or contribute to long-term investments. By concentrating efforts on tasks that move the financial needle, individuals can optimize their time and resources for maximum impact.

The Role of Time in Wealth Building:

Time is a critical factor in wealth accumulation. Compound interest, for example, works more effectively over extended periods. Starting early and being consistent in financial habits can lead to exponential growth. Delaying financial decisions can result in missed opportunities and hinder the potential for compounding. Understanding the relationship between time and wealth allows individuals to make informed choices that align with their long-term objectives.

Avoiding Time-wasters and Distractions:
In the digital age, distractions abound, posing a threat to effective time management. Identify time-wasters, whether it's excessive social media use, unnecessary meetings, or procrastination, and take steps to minimize their impact. By eliminating or reducing distractions, individuals can reclaim valuable time that can be redirected towards wealth-building activities.
Adapting to Changing Priorities:
Flexibility is key in managing time and objectives. Life is dynamic, and priorities may shift over time. Regularly reassess financial goals and adjust strategies accordingly. A flexible approach allows individuals to adapt to changing circumstances, seize new opportunities, and stay on track towards achieving long-term objectives.
Building a Comfortable Future:
Arrival before departure is not just about reaching financial goals; it's also about creating a secure and comfortable future. Effective time management and

well-defined objectives contribute to a sense of control and confidence in one's financial journey. As milestones are achieved, individuals can enjoy the peace of mind that comes with knowing they are building a foundation for a comfortable and prosperous future.

Conclusion:

In the pursuit of building wealth and securing a comfortable future, managing one's time and setting clear objectives are indispensable. The "Arrival Before Departure" mindset encourages individuals to be proactive, prioritize effectively, and make informed decisions. By creating a personalized time-objectives framework, avoiding distractions, and adapting to changing priorities, individuals can navigate the path to financial success with confidence, ensuring a comfortable arrival at their desired destination.

Crafting Your Timeline for Early Success.

In the pursuit of financial success and a comfortable future, the importance of a well-crafted timeline cannot be overstated.

The metaphorical concept of "arrival before departure" serves as a practical guide for those aiming to build wealth strategically and secure a comfortable future. This approach emphasizes the significance of early planning and execution, highlighting the need to reach financial milestones before the inevitable departure into retirement. Let's explore the key components of crafting a timeline for early success in the context of wealth building.

1. Setting Clear Goals and Objectives

Crafting a timeline begins with setting clear and achievable goals. Define both short-term and long-term objectives, considering factors such as homeownership, education, investments, and retirement. Establishing these goals early on provides a roadmap for financial decisions and helps in aligning your efforts toward building wealth.

2. Building a Solid Foundation

Arrival before departure requires a strong foundation. Start by creating an emergency fund to cover unexpected expenses, ensuring financial stability during unforeseen circumstances. Additionally, focus on debt management, prioritizing the repayment of high-interest debts to free up resources for wealth-building activities.

3. Investing for the Future

Wealth-building often involves strategic investments. Begin early and diversify your investment portfolio to manage risk effectively. Consider both short-term and long-term investments, taking into account your risk tolerance and financial goals. Regularly review and adjust your investment strategy as market conditions and personal circumstances evolve.

4. Continuous Learning and Skill Development

A crucial aspect of arrival before departure is continuous learning and skill development. Stay abreast of industry trends, financial markets, and investment opportunities. Acquiring new skills or enhancing existing ones can open doors to better career opportunities, increasing your earning potential and contributing to your wealth-building journey.

5. Strategic Career Moves

Crafting your timeline involves making strategic career moves that align with your financial goals. This may include pursuing advanced education, seeking promotions, or exploring entrepreneurial endeavors. Strategic career decisions contribute significantly to income growth and overall financial success.

6. Real Estate Planning

Homeownership is a key element in building wealth. Consider the real estate market when crafting your timeline. Evaluate whether buying a home aligns with your financial goals and if it makes sense in the context of your chosen timeline. Real estate can be a valuable asset that appreciates over time, contributing to long-term financial stability.

7. Retirement Planning

Arrival before departure emphasizes the importance of planning for retirement from the early stages of your career.

Contribute consistently to retirement accounts, take advantage of employer-sponsored plans, and explore additional retirement investment options. Planning for retirement well in advance ensures a comfortable and stress-free departure from the workforce.

8. Regular Assessment and Adjustments

A well-crafted timeline is not static; it requires regular assessment and adjustments. Life circumstances, economic conditions, and personal goals may change over time. Periodically review your timeline, making necessary adjustments to stay on track and meet your financial objectives.

In conclusion, crafting your timeline for early success in wealth building is a proactive and strategic approach to securing a comfortable future. The concept of arrival before departure serves as a guiding principle, urging individuals to take deliberate steps towards financial success from the outset. By setting clear goals, building a solid foundation, making strategic career moves, and continuously learning, you pave the way for a prosperous future and ensure that you arrive at your financial destination well-prepared for departure into retirement.

Reaching Your Destination Ahead of Schedule.

In the journey of life, arriving at your destination ahead of schedule is a metaphor for achieving financial success and securing a comfortable future. Just like a well-planned trip, building wealth requires careful consideration, strategic planning, and consistent effort. In this practical guide, we will explore key principles and actionable steps to help you reach your financial destination ahead of schedule.

1. Define Your Financial Destination:

Before embarking on any journey, it's crucial to have a clear destination in mind. Similarly, in the realm of wealth-building, defining your financial goals is the first step. Whether it's buying a home, funding your children's education, or retiring comfortably, establish specific, measurable, and time-bound objectives.

2. Craft a Financial Roadmap:

Once your destination is set, create a detailed financial roadmap. Outline the milestones you need to achieve along the way and the necessary steps to reach them. Consider factors such as income, expenses, investments, and debt. A well-structured plan will guide your financial decisions and keep you on the right path.

3. Prioritize Savings and Investments:

To reach your destination ahead of schedule, saving and investing are paramount. Set aside a portion of your income for savings and explore various investment options that align with your risk tolerance and goals. Consistent contributions to savings and investments can accelerate your wealth-building journey.

4. Maximize Income Streams:

Diversify your sources of income to expedite your financial success. In addition to your primary job, explore side hustles, freelancing, or investment opportunities. Multiple income streams provide a safety net and increase your capacity to save and invest, accelerating your journey towards wealth.

5. Minimize Debt and Liabilities: Excessive debt can act as a roadblock on your path to financial success. Prioritize paying off high-interest debts and avoid accumulating unnecessary liabilities. Reducing financial burdens allows you to allocate more resources towards savings and investments, propelling you towards your goals faster.

6. Embrace Smart Budgeting: Budgeting is akin to planning your travel expenses. Create a realistic budget that allocates funds to your essential needs while allowing room for savings and investments. Regularly review and adjust your budget as circumstances change, ensuring you stay on track towards your financial destination.

7. Educate Yourself Financially: Knowledge is a powerful tool in wealth-building. Continuously educate yourself about personal

finance, investment strategies, and economic trends. A well-informed investor is better equipped to make sound financial decisions, optimizing the path to wealth accumulation.

8. Leverage Technology:

In the modern age, technology offers a plethora of tools to enhance your financial journey. Utilize budgeting apps, investment platforms, and financial calculators to streamline your processes and make informed decisions. Technology can provide real-time insights and help you adapt to changing financial landscapes.

9. Plan for Contingencies:

Just as a traveler anticipates unexpected detours, be prepared for financial uncertainties. Build an emergency fund to cover unforeseen expenses and consider insurance options to protect your assets. Planning for contingencies ensures that unexpected setbacks do not derail your progress towards wealth.

10. Stay Disciplined and Patient:

Reaching your destination ahead of schedule requires discipline and patience. Stay committed to your financial plan, even in the face of challenges. Markets may fluctuate, and circumstances may change, but a disciplined approach and a long-term perspective will help you weather storms and continue progressing towards your goals.

In conclusion, "Arrival before Departure" in the context of building wealth signifies the proactive and strategic approach to securing a comfortable future. By defining your financial destination, creating a roadmap, prioritizing savings and investments, and embracing financial discipline, you can accelerate your journey towards financial success. Remember, the key lies in consistent effort, informed decision-making, and staying the course even when the path seems challenging.

Methods for efficiently Managing your Time:

In the fast-paced world we live in, time is a precious commodity that often slips away unnoticed. Effectively managing your time is not just about being productive; it's a crucial aspect of building wealth and ensuring a comfortable future. In this guide, we will explore methods for efficiently managing your time, aligning with the philosophy of "arrival before departure" in the pursuit of financial well-being.

1. Prioritize and Plan

The foundation of efficient time management lies in prioritization and planning. Begin by identifying your long-term financial goals, breaking them down into smaller, manageable tasks. Allocate specific time slots for each task, focusing on high-priority activities that contribute directly to your wealth-building objectives. Creating a daily or weekly schedule helps you stay organized and ensures that essential tasks are not overlooked.

2. Time Blocking for Financial Tasks

Adopt the practice of time blocking, where you allocate specific blocks of time to similar activities. Dedicate a portion of your day exclusively to financial tasks such as budgeting, investment research, or reviewing your financial plan.

This focused approach enhances your efficiency and reduces the likelihood of procrastination.

3. Embrace Technology

Take advantage of technological tools and apps designed to streamline your financial tasks. Budgeting apps can help you track your expenses, investment platforms offer automated features, and reminders on your phone can prompt you to review your financial goals regularly. By integrating technology into your routine, you can save time and ensure that your financial management remains consistent.

4. Set Realistic Goals

Establishing realistic and achievable financial goals is pivotal in effective time management. Break down larger objectives into smaller, actionable steps, allowing you to make steady progress. Setting unattainable goals can lead to frustration and wasted time. By maintaining a balance between ambition and feasibility, you ensure continuous advancement toward your financial aspirations.

5. Learn to Delegate

Recognize that you can't do everything on your own. Delegate tasks that do not require your direct involvement, allowing you to focus on activities that contribute significantly to your financial well-being. Whether it's hiring a financial advisor or assigning specific responsibilities to family members, effective delegation frees up valuable time for strategic wealth-building actions.

6. Continuous Learning and Adaptation

Stay informed about the latest financial trends and investment opportunities. Continuous learning ensures that you make informed decisions and adapt your financial strategies to changing circumstances. Allocate time for reading financial literature, attending workshops, or participating in online courses to enhance your financial knowledge.

7. Time Audit for Efficiency

Periodically conduct a time audit to evaluate how you spend your days. Identify time-wasting activities and reassess their importance in the context of your financial goals. This self-awareness enables you to make conscious choices about how you allocate your time, redirecting it towards activities that contribute meaningfully to your wealth-building journey.

In conclusion, the concept of "arrival before departure" is not just about reaching financial milestones but also about the journey itself. Efficient time management is the vehicle that propels you toward your wealth-building destination. By prioritizing, planning, and embracing modern tools, you can not only secure a comfortable future but also make the most of the present, ensuring that each moment contributes to your financial success.

Challenge of balancing immediate needs with long-term objectives:

Balancing immediate needs with long-term objectives is a perennial challenge faced by individuals, businesses, and governments alike. This delicate equilibrium demands a thoughtful and strategic approach to decision-making, as well as a keen understanding of the consequences that may arise from prioritizing one over the other. In this book, we will delve into the intricacies of this challenge, exploring its implications across various domains and examining potential strategies to navigate it successfully.

At the heart of the matter lies the tension between short-term gains and long-term sustainability. Individuals often grapple with the immediate demands of daily life – paying bills, meeting deadlines, and addressing pressing concerns. However, the pursuit of these immediate needs without consideration for the future can lead to a myopic approach that undermines long-term goals. Similarly, businesses may prioritize quarterly profits at the expense of investing in innovation, employee development, or sustainable practices that could secure their success over the years.

One key aspect of this challenge is the psychological bias toward instant gratification. Humans, by nature, are wired to seek immediate rewards, often neglecting the potential benefits that patience and long-term planning can bring. This inclination is evident in financial decisions, where individuals might opt for instant pleasures instead of saving for retirement or investing in assets with long-term growth potential. Overcoming this bias requires a conscious effort to cultivate a mindset that values delayed gratification and appreciates the compounding effects of long-term investments.

In the realm of business, the pressure to deliver short-term results to shareholders and stakeholders can lead to decisions that sacrifice sustainability and innovation. Companies may cut costs on research and development, employee training, or environmental initiatives to meet immediate financial targets. However, this shortsighted approach can undermine the organization's competitiveness and resilience in the long run, as competitors who prioritize innovation and sustainability gain a strategic advantage.

Governments, too, grapple with the challenge of balancing immediate needs, such as responding to crises or addressing immediate social issues, with the imperative to plan for the future. Economic policies focused solely on short-term stimulus measures may provide temporary relief but could neglect investments in education, infrastructure, and healthcare that are crucial for long-term prosperity and societal well-being.

Striking the right balance between short-term needs and long-term objectives requires a multifaceted approach. Education plays a pivotal role in fostering a future-oriented mindset. By instilling the importance of long-term thinking in individuals from an early age, societies can cultivate a generation that values sustainability and understands the benefits of delayed gratification. Similarly, businesses can invest in employee training programs that emphasize skill development and long-term career growth, aligning individual aspirations with the organization's strategic objectives.

In the corporate world, adopting a triple-bottom-line approach, which considers social and environmental impacts alongside financial performance, can guide decision-making towards sustainability. This involves integrating ethical, social, and environmental considerations into business strategies, ensuring that short-term gains do not compromise long-term goals. Companies embracing this approach often find themselves better positioned to adapt to changing market dynamics and evolving consumer preferences.

Governments can play a crucial role in fostering a conducive environment for balancing immediate needs with long-term objectives. Implementing policies that incentivize businesses to adopt sustainable practices, invest in research and development, and prioritize long-term societal well-being can create a framework that aligns short-term actions with long-term goals. Additionally, transparent communication about the importance of long-term planning can garner public support and reinforce the need for patience and persistence in achieving lasting positive outcomes.

In conclusion, the challenge of balancing immediate needs with long-term objectives is a complex and pervasive dilemma that requires a nuanced and strategic approach. Individuals, businesses, and governments must recognize the importance of overcoming the psychological bias toward instant gratification and actively work towards cultivating a mindset that values sustainability and long-term planning. By doing so, we can build a more resilient and prosperous future that addresses immediate needs without compromising the well-being of generations to come.

The need for financial preparedness during job changes or advancements.

In the dynamic landscape of today's professional world, job changes or advancements have become more prevalent than ever. Whether it's seizing a new opportunity or climbing the corporate ladder, these transitions bring with them a host of challenges. One critical aspect often overlooked in the midst of excitement and anticipation is the need for robust financial preparedness.

The Uncertain Terrain of Job Changes

Embarking on a new job or advancing in one's career is undoubtedly exhilarating. However, it also entails a degree of uncertainty. The transition period, especially if it involves changing industries or roles, may bring financial disruptions. It's during these times that having a well-thought-out financial plan can serve as a reliable anchor.

Emergency Fund as a Safety Net:

Building and maintaining an emergency fund is a cornerstone of financial preparedness. This fund acts as a safety net, providing a cushion during the initial phases of job changes when income might be irregular. Experts recommend having three to six months' worth of living expenses stashed away to weather unexpected financial storms.

Reviewing Budget and Expenses: A change in job status often necessitates a reevaluation of one's budget. Understanding the current financial landscape and making necessary adjustments can help in adapting to potential changes in income. Trimming non-essential expenses temporarily can be a wise strategy to ensure financial stability during the transition period.

Seizing Advancements with Fiscal Foresight

On the flip side, career advancements, while promising, also demand careful financial consideration. The increase in income might lead to lifestyle inflation if not managed prudently. Here are key elements to consider during such positive career shifts:

Strategic Debt Management:
While a salary bump might be tempting to use for immediate lifestyle upgrades, it's crucial to assess and manage existing debts. Allocating a portion of the increased income towards debt repayment can lead to long-term financial well-being.

Enhancing Retirement Contributions:
Career advancements often coincide with an opportunity to boost retirement savings. Increasing contributions to employer-sponsored retirement plans or individual retirement accounts (IRAs) can capitalize on the momentum of a higher income.

Tax Implications and Planning:
Advancements in career often come with changes in tax brackets. Understanding the tax implications of increased income is essential. Seeking professional advice to optimize tax planning can result in significant savings.

The Role of Financial Advisors

Navigating the financial intricacies of job changes or advancements can be complex. Engaging the services of a financial advisor can provide invaluable guidance. These professionals can help in creating a personalized financial plan, addressing specific goals, risk tolerance, and timelines.

Customized Financial Roadmap:
Financial advisors can craft a customized roadmap that aligns with an individual's career aspirations and financial objectives. This includes optimizing investments, creating tax-efficient strategies, and ensuring a diversified portfolio.

Risk Mitigation Strategies:
Transitions in the professional sphere are not without risks. Financial advisors can assist in implementing risk mitigation strategies, such as adequate insurance coverage, to safeguard against unforeseen circumstances that may impact financial stability.

Long-Term Benefits of Financial Preparedness
The importance of financial preparedness during job changes

or advancements extends beyond the immediate transition period. A well-prepared financial foundation sets the stage for long-term financial success.

Peace of Mind:

Knowing that there is a financial safety net in place provides peace of mind. This emotional security can positively influence job performance and overall well-being during periods of change.

Opportunity Seizure:

Financial preparedness empowers individuals to seize opportunities that might come their way during job changes or advancements. Whether it's investing in further education or taking calculated career risks, a solid financial foundation provides the flexibility to capitalize on such prospects.

Building Wealth and Financial Independence:

A strategic approach to finances during career transitions lays the groundwork for building wealth and achieving financial independence. It enables individuals to not only weather the storm but also thrive in their financial journey.

In conclusion, the need for financial preparedness during job changes or advancements cannot be overstated. It is a proactive approach that not only addresses immediate challenges but also lays the groundwork for a secure and prosperous financial future. As individuals navigate the ever-evolving professional landscape, embracing financial preparedness becomes a cornerstone in the pursuit of success and stability.

Strategies for managing short-term financial demands without compromising the achievement of long-term goals:

In the complex web of personal finance, finding a balance between addressing immediate financial needs and securing long-term goals can be a daunting task. Many individuals often face short-term financial demands that, if mismanaged, may jeopardize their broader financial objectives. This book explores effective strategies to navigate short-term challenges without sacrificing the pursuit of long-term financial success.

Emergency Fund: The Foundation of Financial Security: Establishing and maintaining an emergency fund is a fundamental strategy for managing short-term financial demands. This safety net provides a buffer against unexpected expenses, such as medical emergencies or car repairs, preventing the need to dip into long-term savings. Financial experts recommend saving three to six months' worth of living expenses in an easily accessible account to weather unforeseen circumstances.

Prioritize and Budget Wisely.

Creating a comprehensive budget is crucial for managing both short-term and long-term financial commitments. Prioritize essential expenses while allocating funds for savings and investments. By distinguishing between needs and wants, individuals can optimize their spending, ensuring that short-term obligations are met without compromising long-term goals.

Strategic Use of Credit.

While excessive debt can hinder financial progress, strategic use of credit can be a valuable tool for managing short-term demands. Responsible use of credit cards, for instance, can offer temporary relief during cash flow challenges. However, it's crucial to pay off balances promptly to avoid accumulating high-interest debt that could impede long-term financial plans.

Diversify Income Streams.

Creating multiple income streams can provide a more stable financial foundation. Whether through a side hustle, freelance work, or passive investments, diversifying income sources can help cushion the impact of short-term financial setbacks. This additional income can be directed towards short-term needs, safeguarding long-term financial goals from disruption.

Insurance Planning

Insurance is a powerful risk management tool that can protect against unforeseen events and their financial repercussions. Health, life, and property insurance can shield individuals from catastrophic expenses, enabling them to navigate short-term challenges without compromising their long-term financial stability. Regularly reviewing and adjusting insurance coverage ensures alignment with evolving financial circumstances.

Flexibility in Long-Term Goals

Life is dynamic, and financial goals may need adjustments based on changing circumstances. Being open to reevaluating and modifying long-term goals allows individuals to adapt to unexpected short-term challenges without abandoning their financial aspirations. Flexibility is key to maintaining financial resilience over time.

Regularly Reassess and Adjust

Financial planning is an ongoing process that requires regular reassessment and adjustment. Periodically review your budget, investment portfolio, and overall financial strategy to ensure they align with both short-term needs and long-term objectives. This proactive approach allows for timely adjustments, preventing potential financial derailments.

Seek Professional Advice

Consulting with financial advisors can provide valuable insights and tailored strategies to navigate short-term financial demands. Professionals can help individuals create a comprehensive financial plan, ensuring that short-term needs are met while safeguarding long-term goals. Their expertise can guide investment decisions, risk management, and overall financial decision-making.

Conclusion:

Effectively managing short-term financial demands without compromising long-term goals requires a balanced and strategic approach. By implementing these strategies – establishing an emergency fund, budgeting wisely, using credit strategically, diversifying income, having adequate insurance, staying flexible with long-term goals, and seeking professional advice – individuals can navigate the complex landscape of personal finance with resilience and confidence. Achieving financial success is not just about the destination; it's also about the journey and the ability to adapt along the way.

In conclusion, "Arrival before Departure" serves as a comprehensive roadmap for those seeking financial prosperity and a secure future. Throughout this practical guide, we've navigated the intricate terrain of wealth-building strategies, emphasizing the significance of thoughtful planning and disciplined execution. The metaphorical arrival symbolizes the achievement of financial goals, while departure signifies the readiness to face life's uncertainties.
Readers are encouraged to implement the principles discussed, such as strategic investment, mindful budgeting, and embracing a resilient mindset. By adhering to the principles outlined in this book, individuals can lay a robust foundation for their financial journey, ensuring stability and

comfort in the years to come. The emphasis on adaptability and continuous learning resonates throughout, emphasizing the dynamic nature of wealth creation.

"Arrival before Departure" goes beyond financial advice; it's a guide that encourages readers to reflect on their values, aspirations, and long-term objectives. As the chapters unfold, the reader becomes equipped not only with financial acumen but also with a holistic approach to leading a fulfilling life. This concluding chapter marks the end of the book but signals the beginning of a journey towards financial prosperity and a secure, comfortable future.

Writing a book is rarely a solo undertaking in the world of literature. My sincere thanks go out to everyone who helped to make this book, "Arrival before Departure," possible.

First and foremost, my heartfelt gratitude goes to my family, friends, colleagues, mentors, and individuals for their unwavering support and understanding throughout the writing process. I also acknowledge the diverse perspectives and feedback provided by my friends and colleagues who have contributed to the content. I also want to thank the numerous individuals who shared their personal experiences, making the book relatable and accessible. The publishing team's expertise and attention to detail have brought the manuscript to life.

Lastly, to the readers who embark on this journey with me, thank you for choosing "Arrival before Departure". May the insights within these books serve as a source of inspiration and practical guidance on your path to financial success.

About the Publisher.

"Erudite Publishing" is dedicated to bringing insightful and empowering literature to readers worldwide. As the publisher of 'Arrival before Departure: Practical guide for building wealth and securing a comfortable future,' we strive to foster financial wisdom and provide a platform for authors passionate about guiding others towards a prosperous and secured future. Our commitment lies in delivering quality content that enriches lives and contributes to the journey of personal and financial well-being.